Graham MacDonald

WHELK

PUBLISHING

1994

SECRET CREEK

written and illustrated

by

Graham Macdonald

Printed by the Ipswich Book Company, Nacton, Ipswich

ISBN NO: 0 / 9522649 / 0 / 0

Barge in a Stiff Breeze

TO CARO

WHO MADE THE GOOSE FLY

My thanks to the following for their help and inspiration.

Hervey Benham - 'Down Tops'l'
British Broadcasting Corporation, London
Colin Bloom, Warden of the Walton Backwaters and Hamford Water
Frank G. G. Carr - 'Sailing Barges'
Wesley Downes - Wesley's Publications
W. A. Felgate, Ipswich
Peter Ford - 'Tendring Peninsular Land of Milk and Hunnye'
Paul Gallico - 'The Snow Goose', Aitken Stone and Wylie (copyright 1941)
Angelica Garnett - Forcalquier, France
Maurice Griffiths - 'Magic of the Swatchways', A & C Black (Publishers) Ltd
Steve and Lis Henderson - The King's Head, Landermere
Harry Hopgood - Beaumont Quay, Essex
Joan Hylton-Harris - Woodbridge, Suffolk
John Keats - 'La Belle Dame Sans Merci'
Stephen Knight - 'Jack the Ripper - The Final Solution', Eric Dobby Publishing
Peter Miall - The Charleston Trust, East Sussex
Christopher Naylor - The Charleston Trust
Professor Gillian Naylor - 'Bloomsbury'
National Portrait Gallery, London
Alex Pankhurst - Dedham, Essex
James Pettigrew - Sunday Mirror
Philip Purser - Sunday Telegraph
Arthur Ransome - 'Secret Water', Jonathan Cape Limited
John Riley - British Film Institute, London
'Pop' Ronson - Landermere, Essex
James Sewell - City Archivist, Corporation of London Records Office
Brian Shannon - Vicar of Great Wakering and Foulness
J. T. Smith - Essex County Council Archives
Richard Smith - Society for Spritsail Barge Research
Captain Harold Smy - Ipswich, Suffolk
Tendring District Council
Dr. David Trump, University of Cambridge
Ruth Webster - Beaumont-cum-Moze
Ben Weinreb and Christopher Hibbert, 'The London Encyclopaedia', Macmillan London Ltd
Dr E. A. Wood - 'Thorpe le Soken'

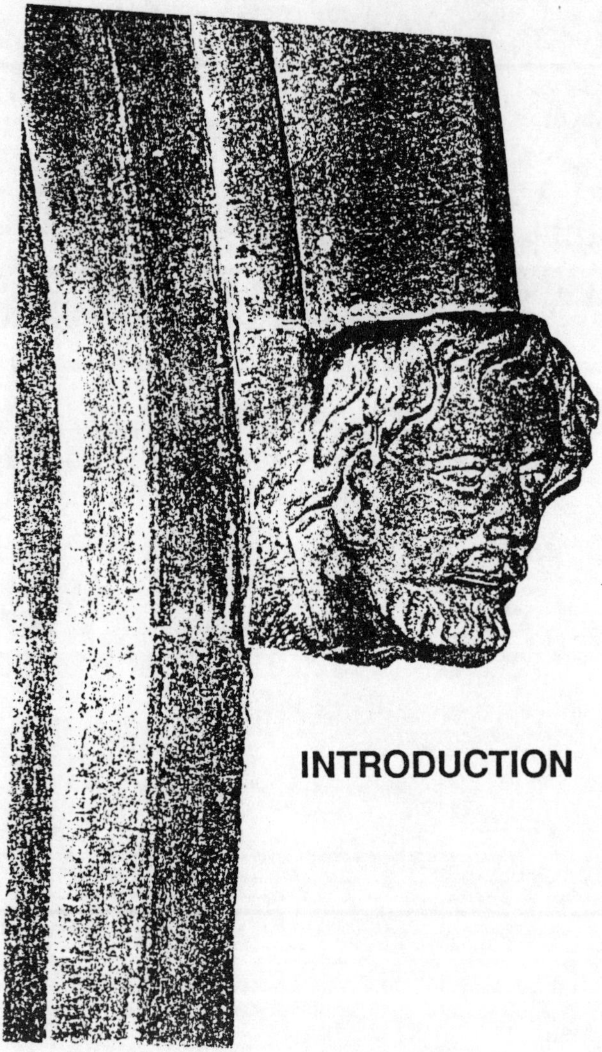

INTRODUCTION

This book began with a lunch in London over a decade ago.

I was sharing a little libation with a journalist friend, Stephen Knight, in a favoured hostelry called 'Vic Naylors' in Smithfield, when he presented me with his book 'Jack the Ripper - The Final Solution'. This had just been serialised in The London Evening News to great critical acclaim, catapulting him from an impecunious news reporter on a travel trade publication to a cause celebre with a handsome jingle in his pocket.

Some twelve years later, after a set of convoluted circumstances I found myself renting a small cottage in Mill Lane, Thorpe le Soken in North Essex - a chicken's hop from the Church of St. Michael.

I was rummaging through a collection of old books concealed in the gloom of a much-travelled cardboard box, when I stumbled upon 'The Final Solution'. I re-read the book with its convincing prognosis that Sir William Withey Gull, Royal Physician to Queen Victoria and son of the parish, was none other than Jack the Ripper, who was now buried in St. Michael's graveyard.

As I digested Stephen's painstaking research into this black pantheon of criminal legend, I became chillingly aware that Sir William's tombstone was just visible from where I lay in the glow of my upstairs room.

The shudder of recognition between accuser and accused triggered something within which compelled me to uncover further facts about Gull and his life at Thorpe le Soken. This search lead me inevitably to Landermere where Gull had lived as a boy.

This humble hamlet, with its crumbling inn and clutch of cottages is hard by Landermere Creek, Beaumont Quay and Skippers Island - a magical area I have called 'Secret Creek' - a mere appendage to The Backwaters.

It is one of the last wild places in Britain, an expanse of grass and reeds that merges with the saltings and the restless sea.

From this solitary, unprepossessing place, is unleashed a plethora of larger-than-life characters and legends, which are now captured, in part, in these pages.

Stephen Knight has now sadly died, and I often wonder whether he finally confronted Sir William in that great ether of the after-life and whether he was able to prove irrevocably that **his** final solution was indeed **the** final solution.

Graham Macdonald
Thorpe le Soken,
July 1993

St Michaels Church, Thorpe le Soken

CONTENTS

ILLUSTRATIONS

SECRET CREEK

OLD BONES AND GHOSTS

The Knight of Landermere - Barges, Bargemen and Hufflers - Farmer Hopgood and Captain Smy - Privateer Munnings - Old London Bridge - Skippers Island

The Knight of Landermere

O, what can ail thee, Knight-at-arms
Alone and palely loitering?
The sedge has withered from the lake
And no birds sing - John Keats

Long before the tales that follow, was a knight in the 13th Century who trudged the 'Secret Creek' and smelled its marsh mists.

Known as 'The Knight of Landermere', his true identity remains a mystery, but his effigy now rests in the South arcade of the chancel of St. Michael's Church, Thorpe le Soken. For over 700 years he has lain impassively watching the monumental events that have shaped our history.

His effigy was first described in Symond's heraldic 'Survey of Essex' in 1640.

The Knight of Landermere, St Michael's Church, Thorpe le Soken

Bones of 'The Rose'
Beaumont-cum-Mose

Barges, bargemen and hufflers

The broken bones of 'The Rose' an old barge half submerged in the muddy marshes of Beaumont Quay bear testimony to an era that was once throbbing with commercial hustle and bustle.

The yarns and shanties of the bargemen and hufflers still seem to permeate these saltings and mingle with the cries of sea birds that proliferate the Creek.

Once, such barges as 'Beaumont Belle', 'Veronica', 'Hector', 'Gleaner', and 'Water Lily', were an integral part of this rustic scene and there was scarcely a time when their canted spreets didn't creep into the landscape.

Sailing barges dominated the East Coast for a hundred years (from the middle of the 19th Century to the middle of the 20th Century) and the interdependence of plough and sail on the rural economy during this period was considerable.

Hervey Benham wrote intimately and authoritatively about barges and bargemen and captured the spirit of those lost decades in his book 'Down Tops'l'.

In it, he dedicates a chapter to the Backwaters, the ditch- crawlers, days of pitch and poke, Walton archipelago and hufflers.

The latter, were a rare breed of salty dogs that could gently persuade a 120 ton sailing vessel up a meandering and tortuous creek in fierce headwinds - without a tug. Their name was derived from the way they used to position themselves on the 'huff' or bow of swimhead lighters.

"Often retired bargemen themselves", says Benham, "they were respected and well-loved friends of sailormen, versed in every subtlety of the waters, using all manner of ways to coax and humour a barge into tight corners".

David Lay, who lived and served at Landermere is perhaps the best known of the Essex hufflers.

"Good morning my dear", he would quip rowing up in his punt. "You got here then?".

His punt made fast, he would then proceed to jig on the barge deck which, together with a colourful flow of chatter, would not cease until the job of piloting was done.

"Perched up along remote sea walls and tucked away in tiny docks, the barges were often beneaped", adds Benham, "but David Lay came to them on every tide - day or night, paddling his punt, whether there was any real chance of getting away or not."

David Lay, like many of his fellow hufflers, is long gone and there are few alive that have any personal recollection of life in Secret Creek.

'Veronica' at Beaumont Quay

Farmer Hopgood and Captain Smy

78-year-old Harry Hopgood is one such person who farmed in the area for four decades. He came to Beaumont as a boy of eight and remembers the barges and old quay well.

"Beside the quay", he told me, "was a large granary which was built of brick and slate and housed stables. Alongside this, was a coal store for 600 tons, a lime kiln and a Barn near a man-made channel called 'The Cut'. The last two buildings are still there today.

"The Cut Barn provided extra storage and in those days the door was opposite the creek so that cargoes could be unloaded straight from the barges. The lime kiln was also fed directly from the barges bringing chalk from Kent.

"In the 1920's the granary and offices were converted into two houses and I lived there from 1941 until 1950 before the devastating East Coast floods of 1953.

"During its history, this was a very busy area. I remember an old skipper, 'Juggy' Webb, who frequently sailed these waters saying he had seen six barges in the Cut at one time. This included Landermere Hard, which was used mainly for loading bundles of straw for London and returning with manure from stables in the city. It was 'Juggy' who once consumed an excess of something or t'other and tried to ride a tricycle on the quayside. He toppled in and took some rescuing amidst the seaweed and mud."

Only three barges actually belonged to the Backwaters. These were 'Beaumont Belle' and 'Gleaner' which were owned by Alan Stanford of Beaumont Hall (specially built for the Cut) and a smaller vessel 'The Hector' which belonged to Hector Stone of Kirby.

According to Harry Hopgood, the last barge to use the Cut was 'Veronica' which was laden with a cargo of flint.

Captain Harold Smy

Another old timer who knew these waters well was Captain Harold Smy - 92 years old at the time of writing, and one of the last of the great British bargemen.

I met him in a basement room in Ipswich, becapped, ruddy faced, sprightly and surrounded by boxes and bags of photographs, letters and other memorabilia from an era at sea that is gone forever.

He began by singing me the chorus from a favourite shanty, 'The Bargeman's Alphabet':

So merrily, so merrily are we
No mortal on earth like a bargeman at sea
Blow high or blow low as we're sailing along
give a bargeman his beer and there's nothing go wrong.

This verse then lapsed into another and several more thereafter!

"Most of the songs are about the sea and come from my father", he told me.

"I used to step dance on a tin tray and I knew an old boy who bored holes in the heels of his leather boots and put some farthings in - He'd do the heel and toe and cor, did they rattle."

Captain Smy sailed the Backwaters - man and boy - for over 60 years. Born at Pin Mill in Suffolk in 1902, he left school at thirteen and helped man two of his father's barges 'Landfield' and 'Cryolls'.

As a third 'hand' on 'Winifred', he remembers celebrating his fourteenth birthday in Antwerp, and at the age of only seventeen, became the skipper of his first vessel. This happened largely by default when he was sealing "little ol' Cryolls" at Ipswich dock.

"The skipper of a barge called 'Mary Ann' was chatting to me father. He asked whether he could take her down Shotley but me father couldn't 'cause he had toothache, so he asks me."

"'Me?', I says."

"'Yes, **you** boy, **you** can do that all right'".

"So, I takes 'Mary Ann' down Shotley to Tony Dermont's Maltings. What a boy he was! Hard hat and all! Someone comments, 'why he's only a boy' but Mr Dermont says, 'He's only a boy, but he done a man's job this day!'".

Captain Smy's first voyage aboard the 80 ton 'Cryolls' (after this early induction into captaincy) was to collect a load of wheat from Landermere destined for Felixstowe.

"When we arrived", he said, "the wheat was still in the field and we had to wait nine days for it to be threshed and loaded."

"Me and me mate stayed at Farmer Cuthbert's for the duration and we drank quite a few drops o' whisky 'fore going up Felixstowe!"

"Cryolls", he said, "got a little bad after a while" and his father took over the 160 tonner 'Beatrice Maud' from R & W Paul's shipyard in Ipswich. Captain Smy sailed this vessel for 32 years, (many of these with his faithful dog Bess), not only around the East Anglia Coast, but as far afield as Cornwall, Devon and Wales. One of his main freight runs was carrying ammunition from Great Oakley to the military base Marchwood in Southampton - a nerve racking and potentially explosive task!

But it wasn't all slog and Captain Smy wouldn't have swapped his life for any other. He sailed in 15 races (notably at Pin Mill) between 1974 and 1980 and won 11 cups in famous barges like 'Ena' and 'Beric'.

At 74 hc officially retired from sailing, but was still rigging barges at R & W Paul's until recently.

I left Captain Smy with his rich memories and another ditty ringing in my ears:

Go down to your grog boys
And be with good cheer
For while there's a seaway
There's nothing to fear.

Captain Smy's 'accoutrements'

Privateer Munnings

In his noble and stoical book 'Thorpe le Soken' Doctor E. A. Wood registers the fact that Landermere appeared in a list of ports and landing places of 1575 which indicates that it was already well-established by then.

"It was", says Dr. Wood, "known as Landamer Lading in 1597 - a place for landing cargo. There is evidence of oyster beds in the estuary in the 1670's but little is known of its history until the middle of the next century when Robert Shearcroft reconstructed the quay to take two vessels".

In 1781, the Lord of Thorpe Manor, Richard Rigby, bought the quay and greatly improved its facilities. This included building some cottages, an inn, granary, coalyard, lime kiln, malting and seawater baths which were 'much resorted to' in these times.

It would seem that estate agents' jargon has altered little over the years as an 1808 survey of these parts illustrates: "This farm is extremely well situated for shiping corn and geting Manure at Langham Mere Wharfe - being only the distance of two miles and a good road to it."

Presumably a snip at old prices!

George Garnett Huske Munnings was clearly a man who relished such opportunities. A great entrepeneur, who won and lost fortunes in his lifetime, he owned, amongst many other properties, 'The King's Head' and Landermere Quay.

Doctor Wood says, 'The King's Head at Landermere was not mentioned before 20 April 1811, when it was added to the properties of Mr G. G. H. Munnings. The following month, it was occupied by James Rayner, but in August 1811 by Munnings again'.

By the Commissioners for Executing the Office of Lord High Admiral of the United Kingdom *of* Great Britain *and* Ireland, &c.

YOU are hereby required and directed not to impress into His Majesty's Service.

Twenty Men & Boys included

belonging to the Courier of London burthen 150 tons, bound on Cruize against the Enemy whereof G.G.H. Munnings is Master, provided their names, Ages, and Descriptions, be inserted on the other side hereof, and that they do not belong to any of His Majesty's Ships: and also provided they are actually on board the said Ship, or working in a Boat near to the Ship, and in the Service of the Ship, and that this Protection be kept on board the Ship. And in case this Protection shall be found about any other Person producing the same upon his own account, then the Officer who finds it, is hereby strictly charged and required to impress the said Person, and immediately to send this Protection to us. And we do hereby direct, that this Protection for the securing the aforementioned persons, and them only, from the Press, shall continue in force for Three Months from the date hereof, and no longer. Given under our Hands, and the Seal of the Office of Admiralty, this 24th Day of Octr One thousand eight hundred and Twelve.

Fee 10s.

To all Commanders and Officers of His Majesty' Ships, Press-masters, and all others whom it doth or may concern.

By Command of their Lordships,

A certificate granted to G.G.H. Munnings for his Man-o'-War 'Courier', exempting his men from pressed service. The complete document includes details of the vessel and the men on board including their occupations, ages, height, hair colouring and distinguishing marks like moles and scars.

Press gangs were groups of men, commanded by officers from Royal Navy ships who were empowered to press men into service. The pressed men were taken, irrespective of job or circumstance, as long as they were fairly young and fit. Once 'taken' it was very rare for them to be released and their families seldom saw them again.

But Munnings was much more than an entrepeneurial landlubber. At one time, he was Commander of the Wivenhoe revenue cutter, 'Repulse' which was the scourge of the smackman smugglers.

Then in 1811, he turned to privateering with his own schooner 'Courier', obtaining Letters of Marque from the King to undertake his new role of plundering enemy ships during the French Wars. A Letter of Marque was originally a licence granted by a sovereign to a subject, authorising him to make reprisals on the subjects of a hostile state for injuries done to him by an enemy's army.

This licence was later extended to privateers to fit out armed vessels which were employed in the capture of the merchant shipping of the enemy.

The holder of Letters of Marque entitled privateers to commit acts of plunder against hostile nations that might otherwise have been condemned as piracy. The practice was abolished by the Congress of Paris in 1856.

Munnings, whose escapades and enterprises took him across oceans as far afield as India, The Cape of Good Hope and Mauritius, lived at Thorpe Cottage, which was later called Thorpe Grange.

He died of apoplexy at Peel's Coffee House in London on February, 9th 1837 aged 70.

Turnstone

Old London Bridge

Stones of Old London Bridge
at Beaumont Quay

At Beaumont Quay there is a tablet on the Cut Barn recording the fact that it is constructed of stones from Old London Bridge.

If history could weave tapestries, then the ghosts within these stones must rest happily in Secret Creek. For each, is imbued with a legend of London that stretches back to 1176 when the first stone bridge was built in the capital by Peter de Colechurch.

That most learned of books, 'The London Encyclopaedia' traces its fascinating history.

> *In the centre of the bridge was a chapel dedicated to Sir Thomas Becket where Peter de Colechurch himself was buried.*
>
> *The bridge had 19 small arches and a drawbridge at the Southwark end. When Simon de Montfort attempted to cross the bridge with his prisoner Henry III in 1264, he found that the Lord Mayor had pulled up the drawbridge, locked the gates and thrown the keys into the river. The London citizens then came to his aid, battered down the gates and let him in.*
>
> *In 1305 the head of William Wallace, the Scots patriot, was placed upon the portico of the gatehouse and so began the gruesome custom of parboiling heads and dipping them in tar to preserve them. In 1548, a German visitor counted 30 such heads on the bridge.*
>
> *In 1357 King John of France rode over the bridge on a white charger, while his captor the Black Prince rode humbly by his side on a small black charger.*
>
> *During the peasants' revolt the bridge was closed by order of Lord Mayor Walworth against Wat Tyler, who took it without a fight when he threatened to burn it down.*

After his victory at Agincourt, Henry V rode over the bedecked bridge accompanied by the Lord Mayor and his entourage and seven years later, his body was brought back from Vincennes, accompanied by the Archbishop of Canterbury.

In 1535 Thomas More's head was put upon the bridge. His daughter, Margaret Roper, later acquired it and buried it at St. Dunstan's Canterbury.

At the Restoration, Charles II rode over the bridge to reclaim his throne, accompanied by 300 gentlemen in cloth of silver, 300 soldiers in velvet, troops, trumpeters, city dignitaries and the Life Guards.

The next year, the custom of displaying the heads of traitors was discontinued.

A competition for designs to replace the old bridge as part of the Port of London improvements was held in 1799 - 1801. In 1823 - 31 a new bridge of five stone arches upstream from the old bridge was built by Sir John Rennie.

Landermere Quay

Skippers Island

'GameBird' off Skippers Island

Sea hog's fennel, Foesell's bush cricket, Ben Fisher's estuarine moth, the Essex Skipper, and the Rough-legged Buzzard are just a few of the inhabitants and regular visitors to Skippers Island.

This magical, unspoilt place in the midst of Secret Creek, is a naturalist's utopia.

Flanked by the waters of Landermere and Kirby Creeks, this 233 acre 'gem' is now an important nature reserve administered by the Essex Wildlife Trust. Once, sheep were swum across shallow causeways and grazed on its rich, coarse grass.

Brent geese, redshanks, godwits, gulls, kestrels, oyster catchers, avocets, terns, herons, storks and many other wild birds are attracted to this sanctuary because of its isolation and bountiful saltings.

Skippers Island has suffered something of a split-personality complex during its history. For centuries, it was called Holmes Island (as depicted in the maps of John Oliver (1696), Chapman and Andre (1777) and Greenwood (1824)) and it was only in 1805 that it assumed the title, Skippers Island. This transition of name apparently occurred in 1805 when the area was surveyed by the Army which were preparing for a Napoleonic invasion. It was then called Skippers or Holmes Island, but by the 1875 Ordnance Survey, was recorded solely as Skippers.

There is one fanciful legend that claims the name was derived from the old sailing barges that would pause to allow their masters to 'skip-off' with contraband on their way to Landermere Wharf. The mate would then berth and clear customs before the skipper rejoined his vessel under cover of darkness.

In his book 'Tendring Peninsular - Land of Milk and Hunnye', Peter Ford reckons the more likely explanation is that Skippers is so called because of the wealthy Skipper family who lived at Kirby in the mid to late 18th Century.

Remants of the old barge 'Alpha', Skippers Island.

"The Skipper Family", he says, "was reputed to have been well respected and well known in the area. It is plausible therefore, that the name change from Holmes to Skippers Island was partly due to a sign of respect, as well as an indication of a well-established and descriptive local designation - John Skipper's Island soon becoming Skippers Island."

"So, although barge skippers may well have enjoyed 'skipping off' ship to shelter on the island with ankers of smuggled brandy, they cannot be credited with the change of name, much as the story appeals!"

When I first visited Skippers Island, it was an experience that perfectly encapsulated all the beauty and wonderment of 'Secret Creek'.

I was taken there on a crisp, autumnal day by the Warden of the Backwaters and Hamford Waters, Colin Bloom, in his launch, 'Gamebird'.

Colin comes from a long line of local sailors who include his uncle, Frank Bloom, who was Warden on these waters for seven years, and his grandfather, 'Puggy' Bloom, who was at one time Pilot for Landermere, Kirby and Walton.

With her engine burbling on a choppy sea, 'Gamebird' took us from Titchmarsh's Marina at Walton, into The Twizzle, along Walton Channel and Hamford Water, then into Kirby Creek where we moored alongside Skippers Island, opposite Batt's Hall.

Silence, save for a gentle lapping about our stern and the convivial cry of a single redshank overhead.

While savouring a coffee and the sight of this haunting place, a flock of the first Brent Geese touched down silently on the swelling tide.

Once ashore, we visited 'Fred's Hut' (named after the once-owner Fred Williams); saw the burnt-out hulk of his old barge 'Alpha'; strolled amongst the prolific blackberry bushes, salsify, horsetail, corn cockles, yellow horned poppies and sea hog's fennel and wallowed in the atmosphere of this unique, solitary and wondrous island that appears to hang on the very edge of time.

Colin Bloom nudging into Skippers

FREDERICK THE GREAT AND THE NOBLE GULL

The Essex Giant - Schooner Villa - Sir William Withey Gull - Prince 'Eddy' - Walter Sickert - Annie Crook - The Whitechapel murders - Jack the Ripper.

The Essex Giant

The ragged track to Landermere Quay splices through fields of barley and wheat that are reckoned to be among the finest in the land.

It begins near a small pond off the Walton Road which skims past hunched barns, resplendent Landermere Hall and a row of old farm workers' cottages that were once reputed to include among their ranks, a wooden Saxon church and a fascinating home that was built around the hulk of an old boat.

Both the church and the 'old boat house' which was called, 'Schooner Villa', are long gone.

Local historian, 'Pop' Ronson who lives in one of the old cottages, told me that she believes Frederick Kempster, The Essex Giant, lived in 'Schooner Villa' because she had seen several references to his living in a boat and this was the only one of its kind in the area. Tinges of David Copperfield!

Kempster, who at eight-feet-four-and-a-half-inches was reported to be the tallest man in Britain, still features in 'The Guinness Book of Records'.

Born in 1888, his burning ambition was to be 10ft. tall. His height was average for his age until he was 12 then he suddenly sprouted and at the age of 25 was nearly 8 foot tall and 25 stone.

Standing upright in the average house was exceedingly difficult for him (as was ordinary work because tools were not designed for his extraordinary size) and he decided to capitalise on his height by performing in his own one-man show.

This took him the length and breadth of the country but he often returned to visit his mother and sister at 'Schooner Villa'.

Frederick Kempster shaking hands with the landlady of 'The Kings Head'.

Such was his size that he could easily shake hands with people from upstairs windows, and soldiers pictured with him during the First World War, scarcely reached his elbow.

At the outbreak of war he had the misfortune to be touring Germany and was interned in a prison camp.

'Frederick the Great' died in Blackburn, Lancashire, in 1918 aged 30. Because of his size, his coffin had to be manhandled through a hotel room window and he was buried in an extra-large 10ft. grave.

The Noble Gull

The swirling mists of Landermere shroud many a secret but none so compelling as that of Jack the Ripper. A far cry from the foggy gas lit streets of Whitechapel, this tiny enclave on the Essex Backwaters became unwittingly enmeshed in a web of a gruesome drama that has tantalised and terrorised for over a century.

For, it was here, in this unprepossessing place, that William Withey Gull (later Physician Royal to Queen Victoria), lived as a boy at Landermere.

He was, through a set of macabre circumstances to become not merely a player, but the protagonist in the world's most enduring criminal legend - Jack the Ripper.

He was born in the parish of St. Leonard, Colchester, on 31st December, 1816. The son of John Gull, a barge owner on the river Lea, he was the youngest of eight children, two of whom died in infancy.

The family moved to Thorpe le Soken in 1820 and when his father died of cholera seven years later, and the arduous task of bringing up six children fell to his mother, Elizabeth. In 1832, Mrs Gull moved with her family to Landermere - which was part of an estate owned by Guy's Hospital in London.

Adjacent to the estate was the parish of Beaumont, whose rector, Mr Harrison was the nephew of the Treasurer of Guy's Hospital, Benjamin Harrison.

Knight says, "It seems the rector was deeply fond of Mrs Gull, and one of the affectionate acts in his gentlemanly and selfless wooing was to welcome young William to the Rectory every other day for private tuition. The influence of Rector Harrison gradually eroded the boy's adolescent desire to go to sea, and instilled in him a firm ambition to become a doctor."

William Gull's
Cottage at Landermere Quay

Once he had made up his mind to enter medicine, nothing could discourage him and just before his twenty-first birthday, he finally met Benjamin Harrison and was accepted as a student at Guy's.

He was a brilliant scholar winning major prizes during his years of study for a B.A. Medicine which he attained in 1841. He achieved honours in Physiology and Comparative Anatomy, in Surgery and Medicine.

In 1842, he was appointed to teach Materia Medica at Guy's and in 1843 became lecturer on Natural Philosophy at the hospital.

Three years later, he gained a gold medal in his M.D. Degree at the University of London - the highest honour in medicine the University could bestow.

For the next ten years at Guy's he was lecturer on Physiology and Comparative Anatomy and was elected Fullerian Professor of Physiology at the Royal Institution of Great Britain and became a Fellow of the Royal College of Physicians and Resident Physician at Guy's.

Gull became a household name after 1871, when he attended the Prince of Wales who had contracted typhoid whilst visiting Sandringham. The Prince recovered under Gull's ministrations, and in 1872 he was created a baronet and appointed the Prince of Wales's regular physician. He later became Physician Extraordinary, then subsequently Physician in Ordinary, to Queen Victoria.

In his intriguing book, Stephen Knight links Gull inextricably with the horrific murders of five London prostitutes.

The source of the story, which accuses the Royal Physician of destroying the evidence of Royal indiscretions, stems from the son of the famous painter, Walter Sickert. At the age of 14, he claims, his father told this tale:

Queen Victoria's grandson, Prince 'Eddy' Duke of Clarence, was put under the influence of the painter Walter Sickert 'to broaden his outlook', and rented rooms in 'Bohemia', Cleveland Street, London. The Prince fell in love with an attractive but illiterate shop girl, Annie Crook who did some modelling for the painter. Annie became pregnant, and at Marylebone Workhouse, gave birth to a girl, Alice Margaret.

The affair was a closely guarded secret. Annie continued to live at 6 Cleveland Street in the basement and served in the shop with Mary Kelly, employed as the child's nanny.

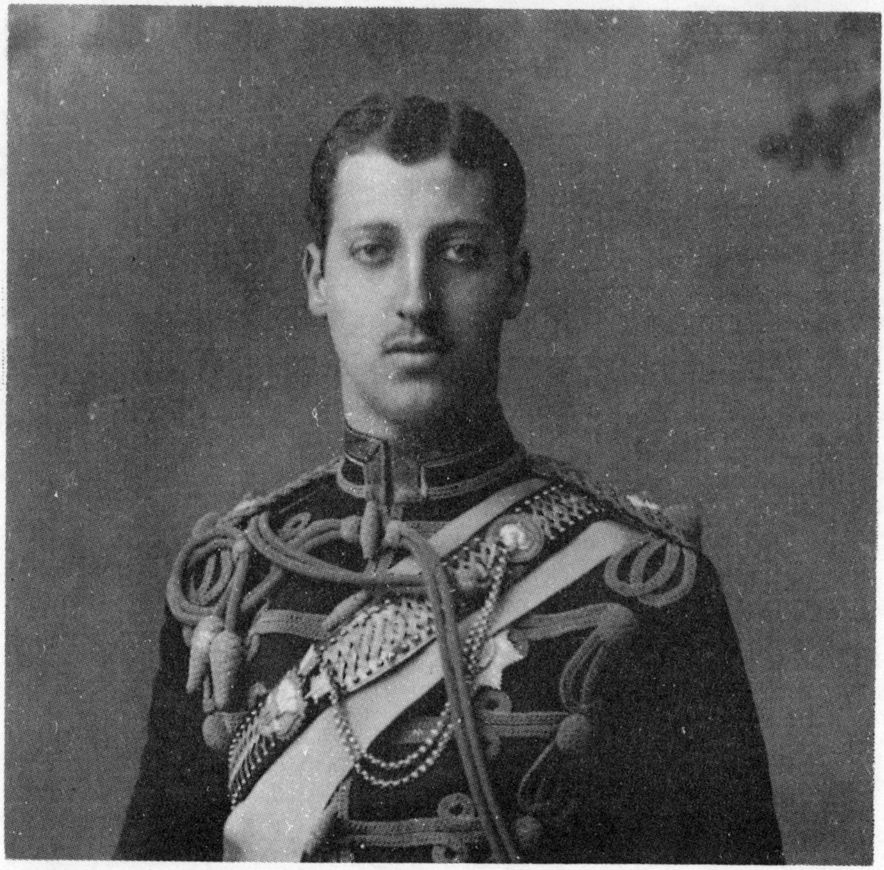

Prince Eddy about 1890
Hulton Deutsch Collection

Eddy and Annie went through a wedding ceremony, but tongues inevitably began to wag and the Queen ordered Prime Minister Salisbury to deal with what was clearly an explosive situation. Cleveland Street was raided by the police and Eddy was despatched back to Court and placed under strict supervision. Annie was confined to 156 days at Guy's Hospital and later to workhouses and hospitals until, 32 years later she died, insane.

Mary Kelly fled back to the East End of London, but shared her secret with several harlots, who devised a plan of blackmail.

So, the Court physician, having signed the certificate to put Annie Crook away, was charged with eliminating the prostitute witnesses including:

Ann Nichol, whose throat was cut and body brutally mutilated; Ann Chapman whose intestines were severed from their mesenteric attachments and lifted out of the body and placed on the shoulder of the corpse; Elizabeth Stride whose throat was slit; Catherine Eddowes who was killed by mistake and Mary Kelly, who was tracked down in her own room, murdered, and the body placed at some risk, in another place.

All evidence of the Royal scandal was thus eliminated, according to Sickert, by a conspiracy master-minded by the Royal Physician.

Knight recalls a visit to Gull's grave at Thorpe le Soken which has some interesting implications.

> *In March 1974, I visited Gull's grave in St Michael's Churchyard, a grave which he is supposed to share with his wife. By coincidence his headstone bears the same text as the wall of the Working Lads Institute at Whitechapel where the first two Ripper inquests were held; 'What doth the Lord require of thee, but to do justly, and to love mercy, and to walk humbly with thy God?' It was Gull's favourite biblical text.*

Sir William Gull
Hulton Deutsch Collection

I was shown the grave by an affable verger, a sixty-six year old pillar of the Church called Mr Downes.

As we gazed at the grave it brought to mind the story of Dr Howard, which said the eminent physician who was Jack the Ripper had been confined in an asylum while a sham death and burial was staged. Downes had no idea I was interested in Gull, so I was astonished when he said, 'This is a large grave, about twelve feet by nine, too large for two people. Some say more than two people are buried here. It's big enough for three, that grave.'

Then, half jokingly, he mused, 'of course it's possible somebody else is buried there, without anyone knowing who.'

There is every indication that Gull was the doctor referred to by Howard and that he was committed to an asylum under the name Mason. Meanwhile, a bogus funeral was gone through and a coffin filled with stones was lowered into the grave. But what happened when Gull actually died? Either he was buried elsewhere under the name Mason or pressure was brought to bear and he was secretly laid in his rightful grave, taking up the third place in the grave for two.

Gull's grave
St Michael's Church

MUSES OF THE MARSHES

The King's Head - Nigel Henderson - The Bloomsburys
Angelica Garnett - The Snow Goose - Arthur Ransome
Maurice Griffiths

'Broadie' at Beaumont Quay

The Kings Head

There can have been few inns more idylically located than 'The Kings Head'

Squat by Landermere Quay, it is a decadent, secretive, brooding place that overlooks the tufted creek and is often enfurled in marsh mists.

One feels it has seen and known much it its time, but like a trusted confidante, utters narry a word.

The pirates, bargemen, farmers, brigands, smugglers, swashbucklers and wenches that quaffed their ale, sank their pootles of burnt sac and spun their yarns within its walls, can only be imagined.

It ceased being a public house in 1913 when it lost it's licence because it was a notorious smugglers' haunt.

Nigel Henderson

Today, it is owned by two friends, Lis and Stephen Henderson in whose conservatory I have often shared a meal amidst the remnants of Stephen's father's creations. Nigel Henderson, was something of a tour-de-force in the early 1950's when he combined with Eduardo Paolozzi (who also lived for a time at Landermere) to produce some of the most powerful and provocative images of that era. Some of his work is still housed in the Tate.

A contemporary, Frank Whitford, who was instrumental in staging an exhibition for Henderson at Kettle's Yard Gallery, Cambridge, said:

> *Henderson's work starts not so much with the film in the camera, as in the darkroom where, often literally anything will do to make a print; not only a dirty, torn or crumpled negative, but also the most unlikely objects which, when placed directly on light sensitive paper and exposed, work themselves as negatives. Bottles, torn tissue paper, string, wool and large blocks of ice have all been pressed into service.*
>
> *Henderson's work, technically highly original, resourceful and packed with unusual and impressive imagery, is not as well known as it should be, nor is the effect of Henderson's technical expertise and his ideas on some of his better known contemporaries.*
>
> *Hamilton's 'Growth and Form' exhibition of 1952 (in which disparate natural structures were compared) sprang from Henderson's interest in that area. Paolozzi's early experiments with silk-screen were inspired by some of Henderson's and the similarity between Paolozzi's wilfully brutal drawing style and the collage approach to his mechanistic bronze idols of the late 1950's have a great deal to do with Henderson's experimental photography.*

The Bloomsburys

Through his marriage to Judith Stephen, Nigel Henderson became a part of 'The Bloomsbury Group' - that rich seam of intellectuality and creativity that dominated the artistic life of London at the start of this century.

Roger Fry, Clive Bell, Vanessa Bell, and Duncan Grant formed the nucleus of this group of painters and critics, who inspired by the work of Cézanne, Matisse and Picasso, set out to revitalise the 'avant-garde' in England in the years prior to the First World War. Their work then, and subsequently, provides an insight into the English 'post-impressionism movement' which was complemented by writers of the Group that included Virginia Woolf and Lytton Strachey.

Vanessa Stephen 1905
Hulton Deutsch Collection

The Conservatory at 'The Kings Head,' Landermere

Judith Stephen was the daughter of Karin (nee Costello) and Adrian Stephen, whose sisters were Vanessa Bell and Virginia Woolf. The latter, together with Vanessa Bell's lover Duncan Grant, often visited Landermere chatting about their ideas and aspirations in the conservatory at 'The Kings Head'.

This magical room overlooks a mossy sort of piazza surrounded by black shiplapped outhouses, fractured paving stones and upturned steam engine funnels stuffed with geraniums.

It is brimful of Henderson's artefacts including old tiles bearing fantastical sea creatures, photomontages in crimson and burnt sienna, and fanciful furniture. Each creation vies for a place amongst a heady, rebellious jasmine that tumbles erratically about the room.

In one corner is a copy of one of Duncan Grant's paintings of Landermere Quay which dangles languidly from a bent nail.

Through the auspices of 'The Charleston Trust,' I contacted Vanessa Bell's daughter, the writer and artist, Angelica Garnett, who wrote to me from Forcalquier, France, about some of her childhood memories at Landermere.

> *At the age of about seven I went to 'The King's Head' for a week. I suppose the weather was wet since Judith and I spent most of our time cleaning out some kind of barn. We pretended we were going to live in it and were not forced into it by the grown-ups. Otherwise, I remember taking a mud bath, which I hated because the horse flies could not be tempted away from eating me alive. I also went with Adrian and Karin in their sailing boat, but not for long.*
>
> *The ambience of the household was for much tougher people than me. There was no feeling of domesticity let alone comfort.*

All thoughts were, I imagine, concentrated on the great outdoors, which no doubt was very beautiful but pitiless and monotonous. To be happy in such a place, one really needed to be a frog or a fish, or maybe some sort of bird.

'The Hulk' - Landermeer

Virginia Woolf
Courtesy Of National Portrait Gallery

The Snow Goose

Tidal creeks and estuaries and crooked, meandering arms of many little rivers whose mouths lay at the edge of the ocean cut through the sodden land that seems to rise and fall and breathe with the recurrence of daily tides. It is desolate, utterly lonely, and made lonelier by the calls and cries of wild fowl that make their homes in the marshlands and saltings - the wildgeese and the gulls, the teal and widgeon, the redshank and curlews that pick their way through the tidal pools.

Paul Gallico's moving Dunkirk classic, 'The Snow Goose', which starred Jenny Agutter and Richard Harris, was filmed at Secret Creek in 1971. The film crew bunkered into 'The King's Head' for several months and the rumbustiousness of former days once again shook the old inn, which had dozed off for a few decades.

James Pettigrew previewing the film in one of the national newspapers at the time said:

I little thought in these hard-bitten times we'd see the BBC wallow in the fairy tale nostalgic fiction of the 1940's.

But they are making an hour-long film of the most poignant weepie book ever spawned by World War Two - 'The Snow Goose' by Paul Gallico.

Paul, one-time American sports columnist wrung tears of sentiment during those desperate days after Dunkirk with his moving tale of the wild goose and the maimed yachtsman artist who sailed from his lighthouse to pick up survivors from the French beaches.

BBC producer, Innes Lloyd has lined up Richard Harris to play Rhayader the artist. But he's got the real star, a Canadian snow goose - or rather a gaggle of them - safely locked up in quarantine.

They are tame geese, trained in America which allow themselves to be handled and hopefully to fly to order and return when called. Lloyd has picked a lonely estuary on the Essex marshes where a mock lighthouse will be built.

Philip Purser, 'The Sunday Telegraph' television critic, reviewing the film in January 1972 said:

Richard Harris demonstrated that physical malformation isn't in the least unsightly provided its confined to a little hump and a crooked hand kept tastefully covered.

Jenny Agutter's polite high school vowels were quite comically at odds with the Essex fisher-girl Paul Gallico presumably had in mind.

What did she say to the coarse fellows with whom she was glimpsed, twice, at work on her nets? 'I say, would you pass the twine, please?'

Bar-Tailed Godwit

Arthur Ransome

The spirit of that master story-teller, Arthur Ransome, who was so sympathetically in tune with children and their aspirations, is deeply imbued in the Backwaters.

He sailed these waters with a fervency and wrote about the inlets, outlets, creeks, islands, estuaries and spits with a passion which manifest itself in his famous 'Swallows and Amazons' adventures.

Particularly pertinent to Landermere is his book 'Secret Water', which transformed the actual map of the creek and its islands into a fantastical chart of his own imaginings - or, more correctly, those of his young adventurers.

Arthur Ransome after a sketch by the author

Mango Island, Shelduck Island, Peewitland, Tern, Swallow Island, Amazon Creek and Flint Island, supercede Skippers Island, Bramble Island, Horsey Island, Cormorant Creek, Hedge End Island and Stone Point in his Secret Archipelago Expedition.

Here is a smattering of 'Secret Water'

> *They rowed on through a bit of open water, with patches of mud showing here and there. On one side of it was an old quay, with some native boats pulled up beside it. Behind the quay were cottages, and a field in which horses were grazing flicking at flies with their tails. Under the quay some men in shirt sleeves and trousers (native costume) were painting a boat. The explorers landed on a bit of gravel beside the quay, and climbed up it to have a look round from above over the Mango Islands and the channels through which they had come.*
>
> *'That's where we go next,' said the Mastodon, pointing across the open water to a gap on the bank on the other side. 'it's a canal but the water's not quite high enough yet.'*
>
> *John and Titty hurried off along the highbank of a creek and found that this bit of Daddy's map, needed little change, though it did not show the canal, and did not mark the native settlement. By the time they got back, the water had risen another foot, and the others were already in their boats ready for the last stage.*
>
> *Six boats, one after the other, left the open water and pulled into the narrow mouth of the canal. This was the queerest bit of exploration they had yet done but easy to put on their maps, for the canal was almost straight.*

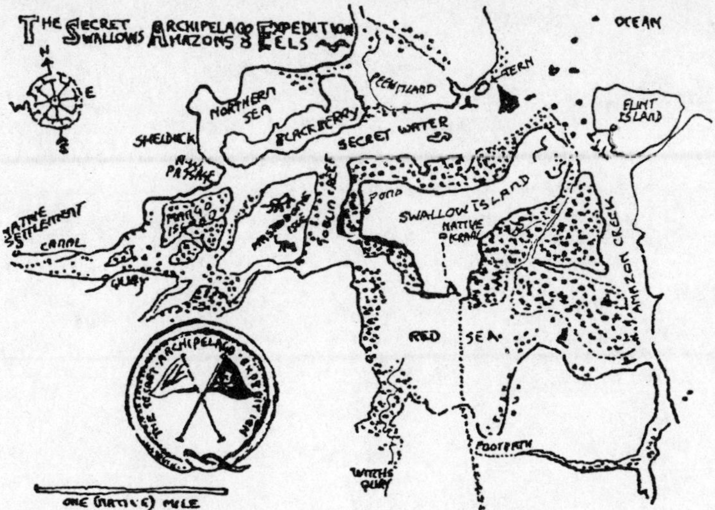

Ransome's imaginery map for 'Secret Water'

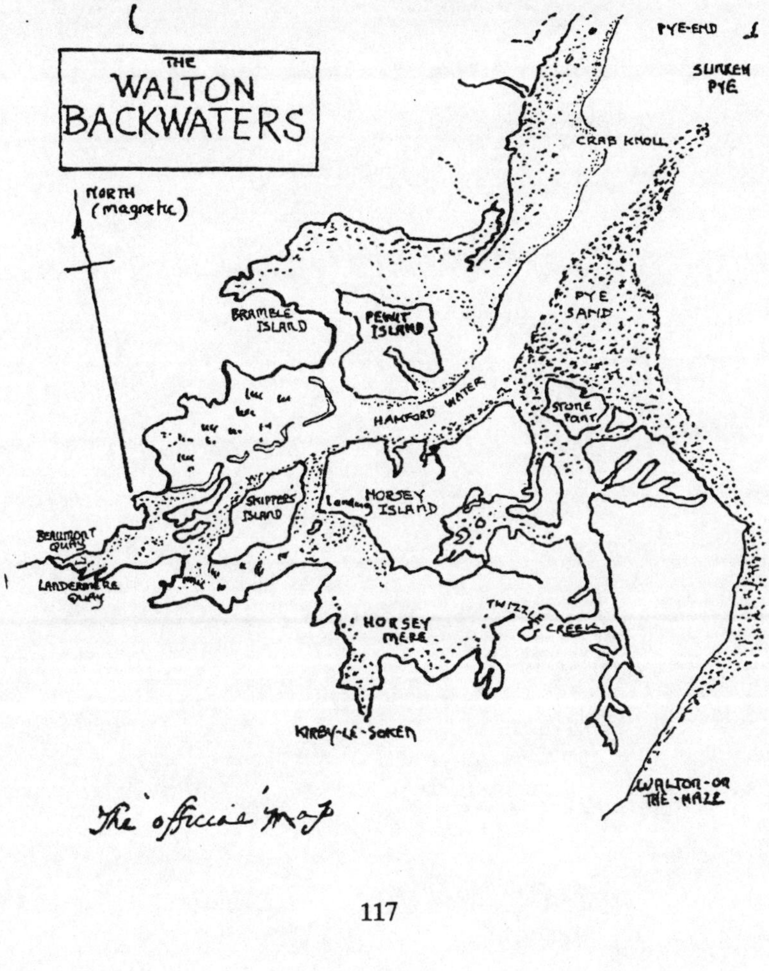

The 'official' map

They stopped when the water ended and they could go no farther, close under some old, tarred piling that had once been a staithe for barges. The water was so shallow that they had to pole the last few yards.

"We haven't been here for ages", said Daisy, as each taking an arm, she and Nancy hoisted Bridget to dry land. "Let's go and see if the cowman's still here."

Close to the staithe were some houses with an inscription on them to say they had been built with stones from old London Bridge. Savages and explorers wandered round them, as if in a foreign country and came to a farmyard, where cows were being milked in a wooden cowshed.

Maurice Griffiths

Another writer who drew inspiration from Secret Creek was Maurice Griffiths whose book 'Magic of the Swatchways' is a nautical classic.

One critic said, "it is concerned with the natural romance of the wild and deserted creeks and rivers and those who explore them in small boats. It is for those who love the peace and the solitude of the creeks at night and the moan of the sea on the sands. 'Magic of the Swatchways' is probably the last and certainly the best memorial to an area which may never be the same again."

Griffiths was at the helm of his barge-yacht 'Swan' when he slid into Hamford Water and Secret Creek. Here are some of his recollections.

> *The wind too, was dropping imperceptibly, and the steady rustle at the forefoot sounded peaceful in comparison with the noisy pounding and crashes of driven spray that had been our lot since leaving Harwich Harbour.*
>
> *Swan appeared relieved at the sudden change and as she heeled again to a last mild gust she whisked up Hamford Water while the red buoy at the mouth of Walton Creek bubbled past, nodding his beweeded head as if to say, 'Oh all right. Don't come here if you don't want to'.*
>
> *And, the row of withies that stood against the edge of Horsey Island waved to us as though they themselves were surprised that any self-respecting yacht should prefer to go up Hamford Water for the night instead of the more congenial surroundings of the Twizzle and Walton itself. But tonight, I wanted solitude.*

Maurice Griffiths –
Author of 'Magic of the Swatchways'

Night-fall in 'THE CREEK'